CHOOSE LIFE IN CHRIST

By

Dr David R Lumsden

NIICOL Publishing

CHOOSE LIFE IN CHRIST

DEDICATED

To

ALL BEING CALLED TO LOVE

THE LIVING GOD

EPIGRAPH

God says, "Search the scriptures; for in them ye think ye have eternal life: and they are they which testify of me." -John 5: 39, KJV, the Holy Bible.

"See, I have set before thee this day life and good, and death and evil." -Deuteronomy 30: 15, KJV, The Holy Bible.

"I call heaven and earth to witness against you today, that I have set before you life and death, blessing and curse. Therefore, choose life, that you and your offspring may live." -Deuteronomy 30:19, KJV, The Holy Bible.

Eight ways to interiorize God's Word, (Psalm 119: 11) that we might not sin against God.
Read, hear, study, heed (pay attention to), assimilate (take in), meditate upon, memorize, and apply God's Word (make part of your life practice) because they are the Words of Life. Believe God because He wants you to have Life, not eternal punishment. Choose Life so you may live. -Anonymous

"The measure of choosing well, is, whether a person likes and finds good in what has been chosen." -Charles Lamb, 1775-1834.

TABLE OF CONTENTS

INTRODUCTION

God gives a life of goodness and joy that He provides, or the alternative, a life of misery and painfulness for disobedience; it is your choice. Choosing the Loving God, and your obedience to His Will are the only ways to enjoy His blessings and to avoid the curses and evil in eternity He describes in His Word. The problem is that many people do not know about or choose the life of goodness and joy. Who, in the world, would choose pain, misery, curses of a living death in eternity? Unfortunately, many are duped (deceived or tricked) by Satan, the most vicious, murderous enemy of humankind. Safety for you is found in The Lord God Almighty, El-Elyon, (Psalms 20: 7; 33: 16; 91: 2; Proverbs 21: 31). You may ask how you can have safety in the Lord of Life? Christ in you will be the determining factor for access to

Heaven in eternity when you transition from this earth.

The words, proper nouns, nouns, and verbs, used throughout this book are chosen to describe accurately life versus death, so you can have strength, hope, assurance, and peace in choosing Life.

Story of Hank

The destructiveness of Satan is shown in his efforts to convince a person to reject Jesus Christ in the face of truth.

Hank was a close coffee buddy of the author. He called late one night because he wanted me to hear more about the Gospel ("good news") of Jesus, which I had shared during a coffee time together. He wanted me to travel to his place to share more with him so as to make a decision about Jesus Christ. I drove about twenty minutes to his home, arriving at about one-thirty a.m. I explained the "good news" of Jesus and answered his questions. I was saddened by his response. He leaned back in his chair and announced that he was rejecting Jesus. I explained that the consequences were terrible, if that remained his decision for his entire life.

The next day, I saw him in the hallway of our business office. While he was walking with another acquaintance, near to where I was sitting with a group, he was swearing, and cursing God. Spiritually, it seemed like an ominous, demonic cloud was hovering over his head. He did not acknowledge me and refused any future friendly conservation. Jesus says that if they hate you, they have hated Him first. Jesus is true, because my friend demonstrated hate toward Jesus and me. To my knowledge, he has never repented (had a change of mind and heart toward God). In eternity, he will regret his choice made to reject life through faith in Jesus. In effect, Hank chose Death because he rejected Jesus Christ.

In the Old Testament, God gives the people of Israel a choice between life and death, and recommends that people choose Life. Death, the alternative, is not pleasant and one will suffer condemnation and regret in eternity, (Deuteronomy 30: 19). God says, “I call heaven and earth to record this day against you, that I have set before you, life and death, blessing and cursing: therefore, choose life, that both thou and thy seed may live.” As you see, God wants you not to perish, but to have life in His presence forever.

Similarly, God inspires Paul, who writes in the New Testament words that apply to us in the present:

“And now, behold, I know that ye all, among whom I have gone preaching the kingdom of God, shall see my face no more. Wherefore I take you to record this day, that I am pure from the blood of all men (Paul preached the Word plainly, understandably and free of any blame by any man). For I have not shunned to declare unto you all the counsel (reproof, where necessary) of God," (Acts 20: 25-27).

Paul instructs spiritual leaders (pastors) to preach God's words of Truth found in His whole counsel. God advises humanity to search the Scriptures (the Holy Bible) for in them they have God's guidance toward being granted eternal Life: "Search the Scriptures; for in them ye think ye have eternal life: and they are they which testify of Me," (John 5:39). Jesus, God the Son, is speaking to people during His time on earth, and like then, His Word applies to humankind today, encouraging them to get into the Scriptures, to search them so the searchers will find the true meaning and importance of choosing life as God instructs.

Many spiritual leaders lie. They present philosophy and vain deceit that cheat(s) and lead(s) people away from the Almighty God's truth. (Colossians 2: 8). They twist the intention and meaning of the Scripture, which confuses God's true message of His hate for sin, but love for the sinner and His desire for humankind to repent (forsake sin and return to God). Confusion comes from Satan, not from God, (1 Corinthians 14: 33). Hearers need to be informed accurately for discernment to be able to make the right choice about life versus death for themselves. They need to know the difference between the truth vs. the lie when they hear what the speaker is saying. Some speakers preach just to tickle hearers' ears. They forsake sound doctrine. They believe that hearers desire to feel good, so the self-motivated speaker will become popular and rich. Many pastors, who say they are speaking for the best interests of their listeners, are twisting the Word of God to make it say what God does not mean. Their message only satisfies their vain philosophy. Some charismatic, liberal pastors express their disdain over Bible-believing pastors, and tell their people, "Oh, we just have to forgive those conservative evangelicals." Therefore, their people are led into apostasy (led away from God). Making the right choice in your life for a genuine relationship with God is dependent on knowing and understanding His Word of truth and life, accurately, (2 Timothy 2: 15). Therefore, it behooves you to read, hear, heed, and assimilate your copy of the Holy Bible, so you are certain of what God is saying and means for you to believe, trust, and obey Him. It is imperative so you make choices that are in agreement with God's will. Even Jesus says, "If anyone will do God's will, he shall know of the doctrine (teaching), whether it be of God, or whether I speak of myself, (John 7: 17). We can ask the question ourselves of our respective spiritual leaders. “Is he speaking of God or of himself?” Any other Name other than God’s revealed name(s) in the Bible, is not the true God, but the name of a false god, or of false gods.

God will hold false prophets (teachers) accountable for distorting God’s words of Truth; distorting His Truth is punishable in Gehenna (the Lake of worms, garbage like stench, and fire). He will reward, favorably, compassionate Bible-believing, born-again preachers and teachers. God approves those who study the Scriptures and learn them so to teach others the rightly interpreted, inerrant Word of God translated from the original Hebrew and Greek into understandable language (preferred versions are King James Version, American Standard V., International Standard V., or the Thompson Study Bible). Be certain you read the Scriptures and discern the truth for yourself under the guidance of God the Holy Spirit. You are accountable to God for your choices, not that of a speaker or teacher. God says that if you believe in Jesus Christ you will not perish (die a living death of punishment in the afterlife). Do not spend a minute more listening to false prophets. Take your precious time to study and to know the truth of God's Word. This is not intended to strike a note of selfishness on your part, nor to show disrespect for the position of a spiritual leader (pastor), but in eternity it will be your final state, heaven or hell, that will be at stake. Choose Life in Heaven, God's Way for your sake.

Many people are led by false prophets (spiritual leaders) to choose a dead god; therefore, they face Death. People follow a dead god or dead gods because they are led to believe they will have an eternal place of bliss under a different name, not Heaven. The problem is that people are being challenged to believe in a dead god or dead gods that cannot show compassion unto salvation that leads to faith in Christ, who makes one fit for heaven, (Jude 22-24). How can you possibly believe that a dead god can be compassionate or gracious toward anybody, forgive sins, or love you with agape love (the highest and purest form of love)? Jesus, God the Son, shed His blood for the remission of our sins, died on the Cross of Calvary for our pardon from hell, and rose again bodily from the dead by the power of the Holy Spirit, so we would be declared by the Father as justified to live with Him in Heaven, (1 Corinthians 15: 1-19). How can a dead god speak, shed its own blood, when it does not have any blood at all? It doesn't take a rocket scientist to figure that out. God says that He provided salvation and eternal life for us through Jesus Christ, whom He sent from heaven to earth to be born of the Virgin Mary, (1

Corinthians 12: 3; 1 John 4: 2). Jesus rose bodily from the dead. He lives eternally. Dead gods can do nothing of the sort. Jesus can, and if He can, He is the Miracle worker, the true Healer, and He forgives sins, (James 5: 15-16). He is God, (John 1: 1).

If you have been misled to believe in dead gods, you are missing out on the real life, a meaningful life worth living that God has provided for you through faith in Christ. Agape love and grace (the favor of God) are characteristic of the One and Only True Living God, Creator of heaven and earth. Humankind, God's crown of creation, was created to have a loving relationship and fellowship with God based upon trusting and obeying Him. Adam and Eve were created to dwell with God for eternity in Heaven, a place of true happiness and joy. However, they fell into sin and became estranged from God. All humanity that followed

Adam and Eve, inherited this estrangement (eternal separation). Sinful humanity is condemned and deserving of a living death in the lake of fire, forever. As Jesus says, if you do not become a child of God, born of His Spirit, you will never see the Kingdom of Heaven, (John 3: 3, 5, 7), nor be known by Him, (Matthew 7: 21-24).

The Fall of humankind and separation from God, came through Adam and Eve, because of Satan's temptation that deceived them into disbelieving and disobeying God. Satan is the source of sin and false teaching. Humankind has inherited the sinful results of the Fall, (Genesis 3). There are many teachings after Satan's influence, worldwide, that lead people away from the true Living God of grace, love, and goodness.

God provided the purification of sins through Jesus Christ alone, (Hebrews 1: 3). There are not many ways to Heaven, as many false teachers say, or many ways to be restored to a relationship of fellowship with the Living God. Is it not fair of God to clearly set out the One Way of His choosing, for humankind to believe and be restored to Him? It was not God who disobeyed humankind, it was and is humankind that is disobedient toward God. Is He not loving and gracious to give humankind the Way to return to Him for His favor; the right to become the children of God, and to be given eternal life (John 1: 12; John 3: 16)? After all, He is the just, righteous and holy (without sin), Creator of heaven and earth, who made and saw His creation, including Adam and Eve, as good. For sin against God, all humanity deserves to suffer in eternal punishment. God says, "for all have sinned and come short of the glory of God," (Romans 3: 23). You have an opportunity to receive God's favor, today, to be rescued from hell, the place of punishment, Romans 3: 24). It is a good choice when you choose God's gift of life, available to you for the asking, through accepting Jesus. Choosing Jesus will provide you a restored relationship with God and an eternity in God's presence in Heaven, won by Jesus for you. If you have Jesus, God the Son, you have life, (1 John 5: 12). If you reject Jesus, you will suffer forever, (Matthew 7: 23). Why so? You did not come to know God, and He did not know you in this life.

The Source of forgiveness, salvation (the rescue from the consequences of sin, death), and the blessing of new life for now and eternity comes as a gift from the living God, through His only begotten Son who paid the price through substitutionary atonement (when Jesus, the Just, died on the Cross, He suffered on behalf of and for the sin of all humanity, the unjust) to appease God. Jesus bought us back so we could be forgiven and reunited with God through a process called rebirth, i.e. being born-again by the Spirit of God to become children of God for eternal Life. In so doing Jesus provided for our redemption, about 2000 years ago on Mount Calvary. By accepting Jesus, we receive and have Jesus, (John 1: 12). When we choose and have Jesus, we have Life, (1 John 5: 12).

Leaders of false religions lead their people into dead, empty ways, far away from Christ, the Way of Life. These dead ways lead to frustration, regret, and death. The following choices show you why a person will be sent to hell. Not all people recognize their need to choose to be reconciled to God. People need to be taught to choose the Living God that by His grace, and His Salvation, immediately your life will be turned around. Yet it remains your choice. God once again welcomes you into a relationship with Him through the blood of Jesus. You are made complete in Christ. This author's book is written to show you that God treats you with fairness. You need to read, listen, hear, believe, and appropriate the truth so you know you are choosing life and not death. Your desire to choose life or death will last for eternity. Confess and forsake your sins, place your faith in Jesus Christ and His work of redemption, alone, and God will give you the realization and assurance, through faith, of salvation and eternal life, (Galatians 3:26). If you choose to follow a false teacher, your life will last you for only your time on earth. In the afterlife, you will suffer punishment and regret forever.

False teachers contradict what God says about Himself. Instead of reverencing God, they curse God or make Him out to be like a clown. Some that ridicule God, make God out to be a "lesser divinity" who created and rules the world. They go against His Word, which is their way of making God out to be a liar. This kind of teaching comes from Satan who made God out to be a liar with Adam and Eve. Two ways of making God out to be a liar occur in Satan's tactics. 1) Satan's deception with Adam and Eve, and 2) when a person does not show a willingness to confess and forsake sin, (1 John 1: 10, "If we say we have not sinned, we make God a liar (deception of Satan), and God's Word is not in us." This is one of many reasons one must believe that salvation cannot occur without the Holy Spirit. The Holy Spirit makes God's word internally meaningful to the hearer. False teachers besmirch God's Word to satisfy their vain philosophy and confuse the hearer. False teachers deny the deity of God the Son, Jesus Christ, and discredit the deity of the Holy Spirit. They defy God's Way of salvation, to their own peril. Satan, through his agents (fallen angels, and false teachers), wants you to believe that salvation is not by God's grace, but rather by your good works, (Ephesians 2: 9). God says that salvation is not of works.

A false prophet says "Jesus failed at the Cross." Whoever makes this statement does not know Jesus personally, and has no business being a spiritual leader (priest or pastor).

Some say that when Jesus came in the flesh, he appeared only to have a human bodily form. This is an unenlightened misrepresentation of the truth. Jesus was sent to come in human flesh, i.e. a true human form of body, soul, spirit, and mind. Choose to believe God because He is real, He loves you, and He wants to bless you far beyond your imagination. By His grace through faith in Jesus, God saves you.

Many false prophets argue Jesus had a wife. Not so. Jesus was pure in His love (agape) for humankind, and had no wife nor children born in the flesh.

Many say that He rose spiritually, but not bodily from the dead.

Some religions say Jesus did not rise from the dead, but His body was stolen from the tomb. Historical fact proves otherwise; Jesus is alive, He rose bodily from the dead, and ascended into Heaven to be seated on His throne at the right side of the Father, where He intercedes on our behalf, (John 20-21; Romans 8: 11). Believe God, do not trust man's heresy.

Some false teachers say that you may be saved, but you do not have the holy spirit in you. Cross check with the Bible. The Bible says that at the same time as salvation, God sends the Holy Spirit into your heart, (Luke 11: 13; John 7: 39; John 14: 26; John 16:7; Colossians 2: 10).

Other false prophets say you may be saved but do not have the holy spirit if you do not speak in tongues. Wrong; this is false teaching. It is important for you to know that you cannot be saved without the Holy Spirit. Speaking in tongues is one of the many gifts of the indwelling Holy Spirit, not the only proof that the Spirit is present in a believer's heart. Believe the truth of God's Word: God sends His Spirit into a believer's heart at the same time as salvation, (2 Corinthians 1: 22; Galatians 4: 6). Not all genuine Christians speak in tongues, nor are required by God to speak in tongues.

Some false prophets twist the Scriptures to say you need to be slain in the spirit, or you need to be able to prophesy with extra-revelation beyond or in addition to God's complete revelation. Many people rely on the word of man and not the word of God.

These False religious leaders call themselves "christian." They are domineering in trying to put a dark shadow on Christianity by suggesting that there are “other christianities”. What a slap in the face of our Lord. Their teachings are lies that mislead followers of their religions unapologetically, to a place called hell, where they will receive eternal punishment. These false spiritual leaders are distorting Scripture, adding to or subtracting from, to make Scripture say more or less than Scripture says. God says that we are not to be deceived, (Matthew 24: 4; Luke 21: 8; 1 Corinthians 6: 9; Galatians 6: 7; 1 John 3: 7). Check out what this author is saying for yourself, and trust in God to help you read and understand the Scriptures rightly, because in your afterlife, you will see the outcomes of your choice that you made in this life. God is not willing that you perish, but that you have everlasting life. After leaving this earth there is no changing your mind. Make the right choice now. Choose Life so you enjoy the bliss in eternity that God has for those who believe Him.

The truth of a future of bliss is verified and promised through Scripture to every sincere believer. False prophets, are <u>not</u> leading people into the Christianity of Jesus, the Christ, who gives authentic salvation that is born of God (1 John 5: 1-2) Jesus paid the price for our redemption. Redemption is a gift. This work of Jesus is good news, because we do not need our good works to pay our sin debt. The price of salvation is paid. Is that not good news? Jesus is worthy of all thanksgiving and praise for paying for our debt to God. Jesus finished the work we could never do, (John 19: 30).

These false teachers do not preach the Good News of Jesus Christ to experience the grace (love, favor and righteousness) of God. You are safe in the hands of God if you read and appropriate (take and use for your own spiritual need first, then, for others). His Word through the Power of His Spirit, by whom you are instructed in the good news of Jesus, will change your life for good. Appropriate the good news of Jesus for your own life now, before it is too late. False teachers teach good works which come short of the glory of God, (Titus 2: 11-14). Good work that is motivated by God comes only after conversion, (Ephesians 2: 10).

The God of the Holy Bible is El-Elyon, the Hebrew word meaning "God Most High," (Genesis 14: 18-20; Psalms 57: 2; 78: 32-35), who loves you and wants you to receive His grace, without your efforts to achieve salvation by good works. Receive His grace as a gift for you, not as a result of your working like a slave for His favor. Confessing your sin and receiving God's grace through faith in Jesus Christ and His work by the Power of His Spirit is how you are born-again. God has set out a choice for you; Accepting His gift of forgiveness and eternal life through Jesus Christ, or death, an eternal living punishment, a sentence because you reject Jesus. God has given us a free will. You choose whether you go to heaven or go to hell.

False prophets lead people to believe in "saints," false christs or other non-gods such as the moon god, the sun god, or the rain god, or many gods. Some give reverence to a non-god using the name of God in their own language, which should only be reserved for LORD GOD, the HIGHEST, the Creator. The moon god, or any variation of it, is a deception of Satan, who wants to draw people away from God. Satan does not represent life; he represents death and eternal punishment. Satan, purely another created angel, is not Creator GOD. Satan, the instigator behind false gods, hates God and humankind, especially true Christians. He deceives, divides, and destroys causing unimaginable pain for people on earth. Some false teachers teach disrespect and the destruction of memorials under the auspices of “no idols,” while they curse God. False Teachers of non-gods are promising a happy eternity, when in fact their followers are being led into ungodly practices and to a place of eternal punishment. Why? They deny the deity of Jesus Christ and reject Him as their Savior and Lord, their entire time on earth. Satan intends human misery, suffering, unnatural death as a score for evil. God has the Power to turn those evil situations into good for all those, who choose to trust and love God, (Romans 8: 28).

Only those people who accept Jesus the Christ as their Savior and Lord, will be granted entrance into Heaven. **Is it not a good choice to receive Jesus? If you desire to receive Jesus now, you can go to the end of his book and pray the suggested prayer of repentance from sin, if it expresses the desire of your heart to receive Jesus now.** If you are not ready, read on for your own sake. The Truth of Jesus will set you free (John 8: 32).

False teachers say that Jesus is only "a god", or that He was only a "great teacher," or that He acquired special wisdom, or He was "one of many prophets," or that "He and Satan are brothers," or teach people to worship the symbol of the goat, or teach foolishly that there is no God. Don't waste your valuable God-given life with these false teachers. God says that the fool has said in his heart that there is no God," (Psalms 14: 1). Do not follow such teaching. The Holy Bible teaches that Jesus is the Son of God, the Way, and the Truth, and the Life. He was sent from God the Father to come in the flesh to save you and me, who are sinners. No other has been sent from God. Those who believe God are declared righteous through faith in Jesus Christ, (Romans 4: 5). Jesus said unto Thomas, "I am the Way, the Truth, and the Life: no man cometh unto the Father, but by Me, (John 14: 6). Believe Almighty God. God means that without Jesus, you cannot approach God nor enter His kingdom of heaven, (John 3: 3, 5). By God the Holy Spirit you are born-again by confessing your sin and exercising your faith alone, placed in Jesus Christ alone. Jesus came to die so we could have forgiveness of sins and <u>Life</u> through Him. To choose Jesus is to choose life. God says "Believe on the Lord Jesus Christ and thou shalt be saved, you and your household," (Acts 16: 31). Whoever believes in Jesus Christ will not die the second death of eternal living punishment. Why not choose Jesus as your Saviour, Master, Lord, and Coming King and be certain of knowing and being known by God before you transition into the afterlife?

As I have said, all teachings of false prophets are Lies or only partial truth. These strange teachings are spread throughout the world by groups that deceptively call themselves christian, but are not. This booklet is the authors attempt to make Life in Christ and the meaning of true Christianity simple and clear.

Some people spread their thinking that they have plenty of money. They think they are okay for eternity. They cannot take their money to eternity. How are they to buy their way to heaven? Some false leaders teach the prosperity gospel, which argues every person that is saved will become rich materially on this earth as a consequence. These non-biblical beliefs are lies against God's Word, (1 John 1: 9-10) and true Christians teach you the truth about what Scripture says about money. Not all believers are necessarily rich in material things. All believers in Christ, saved in His name, have an eternal inheritance in Heaven worth more than money; this is truth. Note, Jesus can take care of your financial needs on earth, whether you are sick or in health, and provide you with His eternal inheritance for every believer, when they get to Heaven, (Hebrews 9: 15, 27). True Christians, while on earth, rely on Jesus and learn to be content with what they are given; which is more than you will have expected for obeying God Most High. He has the best finance system going. True Christians are seated already in the heavenlies, say the Scriptures, and are encouraged to set their treasures in Heaven. If you choose death by not accepting Jesus, you lose money, wealth, and God's inheritance that He holds for you. Your end is only sadness, regret, and a living death.

Some think that believing in God is good enough to get to heaven; they do not need to believe in Jesus. This, too, is a lie. The Holy Scriptures say, "For God so loved the world that He sent His only begotten Son; that whosoever believes in <u>Him</u> shall not perish, but have everlasting <u>Life</u>," (John 3: 16).

What happens if you do not believe in Jesus? Earthly money and wealth do not buy God's love for you to have eternal life. Jesus gives life for all who repent of sin, believe in and receive Him in truth. Many charismatic leaders are living high on cheating their people and the government of money by what they receive through donations, while leading people down the wrong path. These false teachings are running rampant throughout the world. People who do not believe in Jesus, but rather follow after false teachings for their entire life, according to God's word, perish. The Living God explains the special judgment that he has for false teachers: "But there were false prophets also among the people, even as there shall be false teachers among you, who privily shall bring in damnable heresies, even denying the Lord that bought them, and bring upon themselves swift destruction," (2 Peter 2: 1). Their only hope is to return to El-Elyon (the only true Living God), believe Him, repent of their sinful ways and teachings, and believe in the true God's only beloved Son, before it is too late. Don't be deceived, Jesus says. There is only One true Christianity, founded by the One true God, which legitimately shows you how you can become a child of the One true God, to assure you of eternal life. He gives the promise of a home in Heaven for a true blissful eternity to every true child of God. The One true Christianity for which there is the promise of everlasting life is through faith in Jesus Christ, (John 11: 25-26). Only of His only -begotten Son does God say "This is My beloved Son in whom I am well-pleased." (Matthew 3: 17). For the restless soul that is agitated and anxious, Jesus says, "Come unto Me, all ye that labor and are heavy laden, and I will give you rest...learn of Me..., and ye shall find rest unto your souls..." (Matthew

11: 28-30). Take God seriously. He loves you. You can access the one true living God by coming to Him through faith in Jesus Christ, whom He sent to redeem you (pay for your sins; you do not need to work and pay off your debt of sin like a house mortgage).

Spiritual leaders in true Christianity themselves are born again, are genuine preachers of the Gospel of Jesus Christ, and practice what they preach. They interpret rightly, teach, and live the Whole Counsel (instruction, guidance) of God, as led by the Spirit of God. The true God (El-Elyon; God Most High) will secure you so you are travelling the right path, for the right end, eternal life. You are guaranteed a place in Heaven to live with Him forever, by His grace (favor, gift) if you trust and obey Him by following His Way, by faith in Jesus. If you reject Jesus through to your earthly death, you will be sent to hell, (Matthew 7: 22-23). It is your choice.

God is not willing that you or anyone else should perish, but to come to repentance, (2 Peter 3: 9). The choice is up to you and me. You cannot change your mind in eternity. You have the freewill choice while on this earth. If you choose to go to hell for eternity, God will honor your choice, but you will regret your choice. God does not force anyone to believe Him. This short booklet will take you through the ten Biblical beliefs to help you make the right choice to have eternal Life. God's wonderful plan of salvation and how you are secured for an eternal home in Heaven with the Creator of Heaven and earth, Himself, your creator, is what this booklet is about. God loves you and has your best interests in mind to take care of all of your needs and desires, beginning with salvation from sin's consequences, eternal living death. Why are there so many false religions based on their false teachings floating around the world to deceive, divide and destroy people? Satan is like a roaring lion seeking to devour as many as he can because he is cursed and knows his time is short before God puts him away in the lake of fire forever.

Appropriate (take for one's own use) the following biblical beliefs for the best interests that Omnipotent (All-powerful) God has for you. The choice you make at the end of this booklet will be the most important decision you will ever make in your life. Prevention of an eternal sentence to a living death in your afterlife is to believe the Living God and Choose the free gift of Life that He is offering you.

HOPELESSNESS

Hopelessness is an emotion characterized by lack of hope, optimism, and passion. You feel that your life will not get better, nor will you ever succeed in your life. You may feel that life is not worth living.

Are you lost, feel life is hopeless, feel lack of peace and rest in your soul, and you are afraid of death? Do you want to live like the devil and still expect to be accepted into Heaven? That will not work. You need to be born-again as Jesus said to Nicodemus in John 3: 3. Do you want to be rescued now so you have eternal life by believing God (taking Him seriously), thus trusting in His Son, Jesus Christ?

You need to stop for a moment. You need to believe God, agree with God in what He thinks about you. In His hand, He holds a miraculous plan for you far above that which you could ever imagine or dream. Look up to the heavens and unto the hills, all part of His creation, and give Him praise for His handiwork, that he made for you to enjoy. Give Him thanks so you can enjoy true life that God gives by His grace (unmerited favor to you who believe Him.

TO CHOOSE LIFE

A SERIES OF CRITICAL CHOICES DETERMINE YOUR PLACE IN HEAVEN AS YOUR DESTINATION IN THE AFTERLIFE. THEY OCCUR AT THE POINT OF YOUR NEW BIRTH WHEN THEY ARE APPROPRIATED.

1. God Exists

Choose and believe El-Elyon, the Highest God, exists. He eternally exists as One God in Three Persons.

The living God who loves you has approximately three hundred names. God is known by the name God, the Highest, spelled in Hebrew as El-Elyon. In Psalm 97: 9, the Psalmist says, "For you LORD (YHWH), are Most High (El-Elyon) over all the earth, you are raised high above all the gods. This GOD, Most High is the true God the only author of true Salvation. He exists as one God-Three Persons, The Father, the Son, and the Holy Spirit, (Matthew

28: 19; 1 John 5: 7). He, only, is believed and worshipped by true Christians.

2. God's Word is True and Authoritative

Choose to believe that the Word of God is true and authoritative (trustworthy) above all other written word.

All other written word must stand before God's Word as if before a Mirror to see if it is True or False. The Living God is true and trustworthy, living up to His Word.

God reveals who He is in His Holy Word. El-Elyon used another of His many names in describing Himself, as Creator.

He used Elohim. In this name, we first learn that God is one God in three Persons; God the Father, God the Son, and God the Holy Spirit. One God, all Three Persons were engaged in Creation of the Universe and everything in it, of which humankind was the crown of His creation, (Genesis 1: 1f to Genesis 3). Elohim (the same God as El-Elyon; not a different God, nor another God) took six days to create the entire universe, then He says on the seventh day He rested, which is why genuine Christians set aside one day a week for worship of God and rest only. They obey His command to keep the sabbath day holy as He says in His authoritative Word, the Holy Bible, (Exodus 20: 8). God's Holy Word, inspired by the Holy Spirit contains the instructions for how to live righteously and die peacefully. (Note, Hebrews 9: 27, "and as it is appointed unto man once to die, but after this the judgment"). By His Word, God tells you how to be saved and secured to dwell with Him in bliss for eternity. His Word also tells you about your consequences (everlasting punishment) if you reject His Way of salvation.

Rather than have you perish, God wants you to believe Him and be saved.

3. Faith Is A Gift

Choose to believe God for the Faith which He gives to us through Christ, by His Holy Spirit.

Beliefs 1) and 2) are true, and genuine Christians believe them by faith. Hebrews 11: 1 says "Faith is the substance of things hoped for, and the evidence of things unseen." Faith is a gift from God. Trusting God, or putting your faith in God is like you putting faith in a chair believing it will hold you when you sit down. But even keeping the chair solid is by faith in Jesus. Without faith it is impossible to please God, (Hebrews 11: 6). When you decide to put your faith in God for salvation as He has planned, you will have made the greatest decision of your life. Faith is how you please God by showing you believe and trust Him.

Faith excites activity and in faith there is no idleness of religion. In Christ you have a living, joyful relationship with the living most-high God. He holds and protects you, when you trust him through faith in Jesus. God knows those who trust Him. God gives you faith to exercise in Him. Ephesians 2: 8-9 says "For by grace are ye saved through faith; that not of yourselves; it is a gift of God: Not of works, lest any man should boast."

4. All Have Sinned.

Choose to believe God by faith about the Fall and inherited sin by all humankind and what He says about the consequences of sin.

When God created humankind, the first Adam and his wife Eve, His crown of creation, He had created them good. Satan, a created being turned evil, tempted Eve and she disobeyed God by eating of the forbidden fruit. She gave some to Adam, and he sinned, too, by disobeying God through eating the forbidden fruit, (Genesis 3: 1-24). God made it His business to save humankind from their fall into sin. God hated their sin, but loved them, therefore, He expelled Adam and Eve from the Garden of Eden so they would not take of the tree of life. This would mean certainly that they would live in eternity in permanent sin and living death, the wages of their sin. As a result of the Fall of Adam and Eve, all humanity inherited the sin nature. God says, "For all have sinned, and come short of the glory of God," (Romans 3: 23). In Romans 6: 23a, God says "The wages of sin are death." God has a wonderful Plan of Salvation, so those of lost sinful humankind could be rescued from the second death. His Plan was and is that a person is born again of God to have eternal life with Him in Heaven, assured. He sent his Son Jesus Christ to come in the flesh to provide "good news" for all humankind, especially those, who would believe God. Jesus would pay the price for man's sin and buy back for God mankind who have been placed in sin's captivity. (1 Corinthians 6: 20, "For ye are bought with a price {the blood of Jesus}: therefore, glorify God in your body, and in your spirit, which are God's). God says in Romans 6: 23b, "... but the gift of God is eternal life through Jesus Christ, our Lord." God is holy, and will not allow sin into Heaven.

5. God' Vision for You is Great

God accomplishes great achievements for you, if you trust Him through faith in Jesus. Inspired by the Spirit, Isaiah says in 26: 12, "Lord, thou wilt ordain (make) peace for us: for Thou hast wrought (accomplished) all our works (achievements) in (for) us. (The words in parentheses are taken from

the same verse used in the International Standard Version of the Holy Bible).
Choose the God who loves you and has a wonderful and amazing Plan for your salvation and the joy of fulfillment in your life. God's gifts are for all who choose to believe Him.

God is not a mean ogre waiting anxiously to punish you and throw you into hell. He hates sin, but loves the sinner. He forgives and cleanses all those who confess and forsake their sin and unrighteousness.

He wants to give you a dynamic life filled with lasting meaning and purpose, (John 3: 16).
Mankind believes that man's main goal in life is to win or succeed in life. However, success does not mean fulness of joy in your life. God has a life with great purpose for you to find full joy, fruitfulness, and fulfillment.

Believe God for the abundance of joy He desires to give you through His Salvation in the name of Jesus

Christ. Believe God that if you trust Him, He will reward you with achievements of your desires in ways that are far above your wildest imagination or dream.

God says in His Word:

As the Psalmist says of God in Psalm 16: 11: “Thou wilt show me the path of life: in thy presence is fullness of joy; at thy right hand are pleasures for evermore.”

Jeremiah 29: 11, “For I know the thoughts that I think toward you, saith the LORD, thoughts of peace, and not of evil, to give you an expected end.”

John 15: 11, “These things have I spoken unto you, that My joy might remain in you, and that your joy might be full.”

John 17: 13, "And now come I to thee; and those things I speak in the world, that they might have My joy fulfilled in them."

Romans 15: 13, "Now the God of hope fill you with all joy and peace in believing, that ye may abound in hope, through the power of the Holy Ghost."

Ephesians 1: 10, "That in the dispensation of the fullness of times He might gather together in one all things in Christ, both which are in heaven, and which are on earth; even in Him."

6. Two Decisive Confessions

Choose the God who honors two confessions.

A) God says, "If we confess our sins, He is faithful and just to forgive us our sins, and cleanse us from all unrighteousness," (1 John 1: 9).

B) Choose to believe the Living God who sent His Son Jesus to bring the "good news" that we would not have to pay for our sins. Jesus took our place of death for our sin on the Cross of Calvary. In so doing, Jesus redeemed us about 2000 years ago. "Wherefore I give you to understand, that no man speaking by the Spirit of God calleth Jesus accursed: and that no man can say that Jesus is Lord, but by the Holy Ghost," (1 Corinthians 12: 3). God says in Philippians 2: 10-11, "that at the name of Jesus every knee should bow, of the things in heaven, and things in earth, and things under the earth; and that every tongue should confess that Jesus Christ is Lord to the glory of God the Father." John 3: 3, "Jesus answered and said unto him (Nicodemus), Verily, verily, I say unto thee, except a man be born again, he cannot see the kingdom of God."

Best to confess Jesus as your Lord before eternity. In the afterlife, it is too late, you cannot change your mind. Now is the acceptable time, now is the day of Salvation, (2 Corinthians 6: 2). God says, "For whosoever shall call upon the name of the Lord shall be saved," (Romans 10: 13).

7. Born-Again

Choose to be born again through faith in Jesus Christ, God the Son. In Christ all things become new. Believe the Gospel (good news) of Jesus Christ. Jesus is God's Way for you to access the Highest God (El-Elyon) and to dwell with Him for eternity in Heaven.

John 3: 5, Jesus answered, Verily, verily, I say unto thee, except a man (person) be born of the water and the Spirit, he cannot enter the kingdom of God." Teachers repeat themselves for a good reason, to add emphasis to a certain point of truth. Jesus repeated Himself when talking with Nicodemus: "You must be born-again".

When the Holy Spirit gives you new birth, you are spiritually born-again. At the same time, the Spirit baptizes you into Christ, i. e. into the one body of Christ, the Church, (1 Corinthians 12: 12-14). The Spirit of Christ gives you gifts, leads you into all truth, and guides you in godly living for God's glory and your enjoyment of Him. The genuine Christian is said to be in Christ, who gives you eternal Life, not eternal death of your soul and body. God says it is appointed unto man once to die. For the believer, death means the soul which has eternal life separates from the body to be with the Lord, (Philippians 1: 23). The soul transitions from this life to a new world in Christ in Heaven. The soul is reunited with the body, when Jesus comes again and raises the body unto eternal life. He will make you fit, and will usher you into Heaven. You do not need to work your way to Heaven. When you receive Jesus, you no longer need to fear death.

The perfect love of God has freed you from sin and death. You do not become sinlessly perfect, but you are forgiven and given Life. Think of it; no more fear of eternal death (punishment).
God says in 2 Corinthians 5: 17, "Therefore if any man (person) be in Christ, he (she) is a new creature: old things are passed away; behold, all things are become new." You become a new person. You become a child of God, by His grace for eternity, starting from the point in time of your new birth, (Acts 16: 31). We are born -again by believing that Jesus is the Christ, (1 John 5:1). We are saved by God's grace through faith in Jesus, not by our good works, (Ephesians 2: 8-9).

8. Live by Faith in God and His Grace

Choose to live by the grace of the Living God in the new life, hope and joy He gives you.

People born again of the Spirit will have eternal life by seeing and believing in Jesus Christ. Believers will be granted the right to life in Heaven. Are "you" lost, without Jesus? Jesus said that you must be born again to be on the right path to Heaven. If not, you will not see heaven.

John 3: 7, "Marvel not that I said unto thee, Ye must be born again."

You must be born again. You are born of the Spirit when you receive Jesus Christ into your heart. That is how you become a child of God. In Christ, you are on the right path to Heaven. In Christ by faith, your soul will never face condemnation and the second death, which is eternal. Your body will be raised and united with your soul to live eternally in a new heaven and a new earth without sin, (John 5: 24; 6: 40; 8: 51; 11: 26; Revelation 21: 1-8).

You recall that no man can say Jesus is Lord but by the Holy Spirit. Being born again is acknowledging

Jesus, and confessing Jesus through the leadership of the Holy Spirit. Romans 8: 14, "For as many as are led by the Spirit of God, they are the sons (children) of God." One believes on Jesus for shedding His blood for the remission of our sins, taking our place in dying on the Cross so we do not need to work hard for our salvation or fear dying and eternal death (punishment). If we depend upon our work for salvation, our work will always come up short of God's glory, and as a result we will not be known by God in Judgment Day, and therefore, be sent to hell. Jesus died in our place that we might live. On a missionary journey, a, Philippian jailor asked Paul and Silas what he needed to do to be saved. The jailor was afraid of being put to death by the Roman rulers. Paul and Silas said, "believe on the Lord Jesus Christ, and thou shalt be saved, and thy house," (Acts 16: 31).

We believe that God willed for Jesus to be bodily raised from the dead by the power of the Holy Spirit for our justification to live in heaven forever with God, (Romans4: 24-25), "But for us also, to whom it (righteousness) shall be imputed (accredited), if we believe on Him who raised up Jesus our Lord from the dead. Believing in Jesus, who was delivered for our offences, and was raised (bodily) again for our justification, is the basis for a believer being declared by the Father as fit for the kingdom of Heaven. Jesus has finished all the work required for our salvation, i.e. He has paid all required for our redemption (being bought back for God; Mediator mediating on our behalf between God and man; Hebrews 9: 15), so we don't need to work our way to Heaven. That is the "good news": Salvation is a gift of God through faith in the Lord Jesus Christ, alone. Jesus said on the Cross before He died, "It is finished," (John 19:

30), i.e. His mission for our salvation for which Jesus was sent into the world, was complete. Jesus, God the Son, had appeased God the Father on our behalf so we could be declared free to live. Think, perceive, and do not fear. Eternal life is God's gift to us through faith in Jesus Christ. Believe God for what He says, "For by grace are ye saved through faith (in Jesus), that not of yourselves it is the gift of God: not of works, lest any man should boast," (Ephesians 2: 8-9). God took care of everything required for us to be saved to live eternally in Him through faith in Christ. You are eternally redeemed by opening the door of your heart to Jesus, and receiving Jesus Christ, the Son of God as your Savior and Lord. By God's grace alone through faith alone, in Jesus the Christ alone, you are saved. This gift you receive is like receiving a gift at Christmas or on your birthday. Freely, you become a child of God, guaranteed, (John 14: 3) because God loves you and has prepared salvation for you just as a gift.

God sent his only begotten Son to come in the flesh to live a perfect life. Then Jesus Christ allowed His life to be sacrificed as a substitute for us so we would not need to fail at working hard to pay for our sins, but rather have eternal life given to all who believe on and receive Jesus. Jesus did all the work to redeem you.

John 3: 15-17, "That whosoever believeth in Him should not perish, but have eternal life. For God so loved the world, that He gave His only begotten Son, that whosoever believeth in Him, should not perish, but have everlasting life. For God sent not His Son into the world to condemn the world; but that the world through Him might be saved."

Matthew 10: 32, Jesus said, "Whosoever therefore shall confess Me before men, him will I confess before My Father which is in Heaven." Upon receiving Christ, you are known by God.

Luke 12: 8, "Also I say unto you, whosoever shall confess Me before men, him shall the Son of man also confess before the angels of God."

Romans 10: 9-10, "That if thou shalt confess with thy mouth the Lord Jesus, and shalt believe in thy heart that God hath raised Him from the dead, thou shalt be saved. For with the heart man believeth unto righteousness; and with the mouth confession is made unto salvation."

If you confess Jesus, Jesus will make you known to the Father. God will know you in eternity, (Matthew 7: 23-24)

1 John 2: 23, "Whosoever denieth the Son, the same hath not the Father; but he that acknowledgeth the Son hath the Father also."

1 John 4: 2, "Hereby, ye know the Spirit of God: Every spirit that confesseth that Jesus Christ is come in the flesh is of God."

1 John 5: 1-2, "Whosoever believeth that Jesus is the Christ is born of God: and every one that loveth him that begat loveth him also that is begotten of Him. By this we know that we love the children of God, when we love God, and keep His commandments."

1 John 5: 5, "Who is he that overcometh the world, but he that believeth that Jesus is the Son of God?" The new life we live is not by our self-will for our self-gain, but for the glory of God through Christ by the power of His Holy Spirit who God gives all believers at the time of salvation, (Colossians2: 10).

9. In Christ, Made Complete

In the Old Testament God says, Choose Life." Life was through faith in the "coming" Christ. The prophets of God foretold of the coming Christ. In the New Testament, God tells of "sending" His Son to come in the flesh. Having sent His Only Begotten Son into the world to save the world, God, requires specifically, for humankind to "Choose Life, in Christ," as having faith in Christ who has come. No person comes to the Father, but through Jesus Christ, (John 14: 6). God says in 1 John 4: 2, that you may know that He sent God the Holy Spirit into your heart at salvation, because; "This is how you recognize the Spirit of God: Every spirit that acknowledges that Jesus Christ has come in the flesh is of God." God says of His Son whom He sent in the flesh, "In Christ, ye are made full (complete), who is the head of all principality and power," (Colossians 2: 10). You choose life in Christ by doing the will of the Father through Christ by yielding to the Holy Spirit's presence, power, control, comfort, guidance, teaching, and witness in and through you, for the glory of the Living God, (Romans 12: 1-2). This confession is evidence of new birth and substance of true Christianity. Choose to believe the Living God who makes you complete as a child of His when you open your heart to Jesus alone, receiving Him as your only Savior and Lord. There is no other. No one, nor nothing else, is required, nor acceptable to The Lord God Almighty.

John 1: 12-13, "But as many as receive Him, to them gave He power to become the sons (children) of God, even to them that believe on His name. Which were born, not of the blood, nor of the will of the flesh, nor of the will of man, but of God."

Believe God that if you repent of your sin and ask Him to save you, believing in the name of Jesus,

God will do it, i.e. He will declare you as an adopted child of His, eternally secured.

John 16: 23, "And in that day ye shall ask Me nothing. Verily, verily, I say unto you, whatsoever ye shall ask the Father in My name, He will give it you."

Romans 8: 14-16, "For as many as are led by the Spirit, they are the sons (and daughters) of God. For ye have not received the spirit of bondage again to fear; but ye have received the Spirit of adoption, whereby ye cry, Abba, Father. The Spirit itself (Himself) beareth witness with our spirit, that we are the children of God." The Holy Spirit places one in Christ at the same time as salvation, (Romans 8: 15; 1 Corinthians 12: 13; Galatians 3: 28).

Romans 8: 28, "And we know that all things work together for good to them that love God, to them who are called according to His purpose."

10. The Sinner's Plea

Choose the Living God who hears the plea of every repentant sinner when he/she prays the Sinner's Plea desiring eternal life by faith in Jesus.

Believe God to make you a child of His when you see (perceive), open your heart to Jesus and believe on Him. Jesus comes in when you open your heart to Him, during prayer, which is talking to God, because he loves you. Anyone who claims to be religious and wants to kill you by any means is not of the Living God. Believe the loving, living God, (Revelation 3: 20). Believe God will know you as His child because you trust Him through faith in Jesus Christ, (Galatians 3: 26). He wants you to have everlasting life. The prayer of repentance is the first prayer God will hear from you. This prayer has come to be known as the Sinner's Plea. When this prayer expresses the desire of your heart i.e. you truly mean what you pray, anywhere, anytime, believing in Jesus, Jesus will come into your heart and secure you for eternal life in heaven with God.

God promises he will never lose you. John 10: 28-29, "And I give unto them eternal life, and they shall never perish, neither shall any man pluck them out of My hand. My Father, which gave them Me, is greater than all, and no man is able to pluck them out of My Father's hand." You are eternally secure in Christ.

In Psalm 132, God records a prayer on the sanctuary of His place for worship. The Psalmist, begins the chapter saying,
"Lord, remember David, and all his afflictions: how he sware unto the Lord, and vowed unto the mighty God of Jacob; Surely I will not come into the tabernacle of my house, nor go up into my bed; I will not give sleep to mine eyes, or slumber to mine eyelids, until I find out a place for the Lord, a habitation for the mighty God of Jacob," (Psalm

132: 1-5). Read the full chapter to drink in the rich value of God's words.

When you think of David, you think of him as owning great riches, owning a huge palace, affording the building of a huge temple for the worship of God, and you think of him as a great king of a nation, who begat Solomon. Jesus Christ was born of the line of David, (Matt 1: 1, 6). David prepared a place for the Lord Jesus Christ.

You may be thinking that you do not have great riches, you do not have a house that radiates great wealth. You are not the king of a nation and will never be a celebrity known as the leader of a nation. You think you could never provide a sanctuary for the Lord because of all the things that you are not.

The key to David's transformation from a sinful life to a life of righteousness and glory to God, is that David opened his heart (center of feelings; the core of one's being) to the Lord for a habitation. For you it is a matter of a decision. You choose to open (yield) your heart to Jesus. Jesus will come into your heart, clean your heart, make you a child of God, become your Lord, fellowship with you, and never leave you, nor forsake you, nor lose you. When you have Jesus, God gives you eternal life, guaranteed. In Revelation 3: 20 God says, "Behold, I stand at the door and knock: if any man hears My (Jesus) voice, and opens the door, I will come in to him, and sup (friendly fellowship) with him, and he with Me." In 1 John 5: 11-12, God says that he who has the Son has life...."

2 Chronicles 7: 14 says, "If My people, which are called by My Name, shall humble themselves, and pray, and seek My face, and turn from their wicked ways; then I will hear from Heaven, and forgive their sin, and will heal their land."

Will you confess your sin and place your faith in Jesus? Let Him make you a child of God, a new creation so to have an eternal life with God in Heaven? Say Yes and you can begin salvation and eternal life, immediately, as His gift to you, today. If you have already given your heart to Jesus, you can pass this book on to someone on whom you have compassion and would love to see have Jesus in their heart for eternal life. If you have never opened your heart to Jesus, you can pray along the lines of the prayer below to open your heart to Jesus.

*You can pray the following Sinner's Plea. By believing in Jesus, you will have a home prepared for you in Heaven, (John 14: 1-6). God says, "For whosoever shall call upon the name of the Lord shall be saved," (Romans 10: 13). Believe on Jesus. He is the only one to meet your need to be born-again through His Spirit.

Jesus, God the Son, is The Father's Way for you to be given forgiveness of sins and to become a child of God fit to live in Heaven. Read the prayer and be certain you desire to receive Jesus. You may wish to check out the references to God's promises in the prayer or in the book. Then you can use this prayer as a guide for asking God to forgive and save you. When you mean the prayer in your heart, pray the prayer just like you are talking to God, and God will give you the gift of eternal life through His Son, immediately. Instantly you will start eternal life, for which He has given you His Spirit to lead you in godly living, (Romans 8: 14-18). Once you receive Jesus, you are made complete in Him by His Spirit, (Colossians 2:10). He will never leave you nor forsake you, (Hebrews 13: 5); you will never be left alone by Jesus.

If you repent of your sins and receive Jesus as your Savior and Lord, God will give you eternal life, guaranteed, and accept you into His wonderful Heaven for eternity, (1 John 5: 12, 20). God's promises will be true for you, and He will greatly reward you beginning immediately. You will be safe through Life in the Lord.

The significance of the Grace of God and the Power of the Gospel unto Salvation of three people who accepted Jesus Christ as Savior and Lord demonstrate God's love for humankind.

Jesus paid for the wages (death) of all their sin. Jesus gave them the right to become the children of God and they received everlasting Life for their choice to forsake their sin and to accept Him. There was a noticeable change in their countenance, mind, heart, and attitude, compared to Hank, about whom I told you in the Introduction. Hank chose Death. These three chose Life in Christ and were born again.

Story of Jacques' Change in his Life

One Sunday morning, Jacques was sitting attentatively in the front row as I was preaching. I was preaching a Gospel message based on John 1: 1-14. At the end of the message when I gave an altar call, Jacques came forward to talk about was his most pressing concern. He said that he had been avoiding to ask forgiveness for his sins and to accept Jesus. He explained that he was getting old and could not attempt to hide from God much longer. He said he was not ready to die, and asked if I would show him how to accept Jesus (God's Way of Life) into his heart.

We reviewed what the Bible says about receiving Jesus and why becoming born again is crucial in being given eternal life from God. He said that he would like to be born again so he could have eternal life through faith in Jesus. We talked about the sinner's plea in which one confesses his sin, decides to forsake his sin, and opens his heart to receive Jesus as Savior and as Lord where he wants Jesus to take the throne in his heart. He prayed the Sinner's plea and received Jesus by faith. He thanked God for saving him by grace through faith and looked forward to living with God in heaven.

After praying, Jacques opened his eyes with a bright smile on his face. God had changed his mind and heart. God had given him new life. He reached out and shook my hand. He was so grateful that Jesus had given Him Life. We prayed again to give God thanksgiving and praise for His wonderful gift of Life to Jacques. Jacques stayed at the front and did not want to leave. He had begun eternal life filled with joy, immediately.

I followed up with Jacques to help him grow spiritually in Christ. He was a new man, whom Jesus had given the right to become a child of God. God had given him the righteousness of God which is essential for anyone to see the Kingdom of God. God had sent the Holy Spirit into Jacques' heart to seal him, comfort him, and assure him that he was a child of the Living God in Heaven, his Father. Jacques chose life by accepting Jesus, the Christ.

Story of Raymond's Change in his Life

One day during hospital visitation, I happened to stick my head into Raymond's room. I walked up to his gurney to introduce myself. After, my initial greeting to which he did not respond, I told him that God loved him, did not want anyone to perish but wanted him to have forgiveness of sins and everlasting life through faith in Jesus. He did not utter a squeak all the time I was visiting him.

The next day, I went to visit Raymond later in the afternoon. Something incredible had happened. Raymond needed to talk, and was glad that I had come back. Earlier that day, his doctor had given Raymond bad news: he had only two weeks to live. Raymond explained that he was afraid to die. "I'm not ready," he cried. "How can I have this Jesus you were talking about yesterday," he asked. Raymond was interactive.

We talked about the Gospel message of Jesus being good news. He understood that good works could never save him, because he could not move from his gurney. He accepted the fact that Jesus had shed His blood for the remission of his sins. He understood that Jesus had redeemed him about two thousand years ago. We reviewed the Sinner's plea. He indicated that receiving Jesus, the Son of God, expressed the desire of his heart.

Raymond had a talk with God and said that he was not good enough to get into heaven because of his sin. He acknowledged Jesus and His redemptive work alone as his way to be saved. He received

Jesus and gave God thanks for eternal life in heaven. After Raymond finished praying, he opened his eyes and was just beaming. God had graciously given him new life. Raymond had chosen life by forsaking sin; accepting Jesus Christ.

He reached out his trembling hand to shake mine.

We prayed together to give God thanksgiving and praise for His Miracle in Raymond's life. God had changed Raymond's life when He gave Him hope through faith in Jesus who Raymond believed would raise him bodily to live with His Father in Heaven, forever.

In the short time that remained for Raymond, I followed up with him for his spiritual growth and assurance. Just before he died, he had joy in his heart over the fact that he was going to be with his Lord to walk and talk with Him forever. The love of God was shed abroad in his heart by the Holy Spirit.

Story of Theresa's Change in her Life

One Sunday morning, I was preaching a sermon on John 3: 1-17. Theresa was sitting in the very back row of the sanctuary. About two thirds through my sermon, Theresa jumped up and began to shout out, "What you are talking about, is just what I need. I need to be saved right now. I do not want to wait. I want you to come right now and pray with me to be saved."

I prayed in my heart for God's will and He impressed upon my heart to stop the service and take the time to lead Theresa in accepting Jesus. I called for a few of the born-again Christians to join me along with Theresa to pray for her. We went back to make sure Theresa understood what she was doing.

Theresa prayed to confess her sin, and she asked Jesus to forgive her and to enter into her heart as her Savior and Lord. God saved her by His grace through her faith in Jesus Christ. After receiving Jesus, Theresa was ecstatic. She was filled with so much joy that she was shaking hands with everyone who had prayed with her. She was bubbling over with thanksgiving. She indicated that Jesus had taken a huge burden from her. She had the Spirit of God shining in her heart. She had chosen life by forsaking her sin and accepting Jesus as her Savior and Lord.

I went back to the pulpit and finished the service. After the final prayer, Theresa ran to the front and could not stop talking about what Jesus had done for her. She stayed with my wife and me until we were ready to leave the building. As we were exiting the front doors, Theresa reached out her hand and gave us a farewell handshake.

CHOOSE TO TALK WITH GOD

Read the prayer below. God is calling you to choose life through His Son. If the prayer expresses the desire of your heart, then you may use it as a guide to express your desire to be forgiven of your sins and to be born again. It is not the prayer that saves you, but Jesus saves you when you open the door of your heart and receive Him. In Revelation 3: 20 Jesus says, "Behold I stand at the door and knock. If anyone hears my voice, and opens the door, I will come in, and sup with him, and he with Me." This is what is called being born again by the Spirit of God so you may see the Kingdom of God, (John 3: 3, 5) as God promises. Then, you will have chosen Life. If you desire in your heart to have forgiveness of sins and a life worth living, then choose life in Christ. When you invite Jesus into your heart, He comes in, (Revelation 3: 20). This is the proof that you are a true Christian. He will never leave nor forsake you. What a Friend we have in Jesus. Whoever chooses life through accepting Jesus as personal Savior and Lord is born again and will never die the second death. Choose to desire and mean this prayer with all your heart for Life in Christ:

Dear Heavenly Father;

Thy kingdom come. I'm not good enough to dwell in your great Heavenly Kingdom because of my sins. I am sorry for my sinful disobedience and rebellion against You. I confess and forsake my sins. I ask you to please forgive me of my sins. I agree that You sent Jesus Christ, your only begotten Son, to come in the flesh to save me. I believe in Jesus as the Christ, (1 John 5: 1). He came to pay the price for my sins. I do not have to work, be highly educated, rich, young or old to be of Your family to live with You in Heaven. I believe I am choosing life by accepting Jesus. I believe Your

Word (John 11: 26) by faith.). I open my heart (the center of my being) and receive Jesus Christ as my Savior and Lord, (Revelation 3: 20). Thank you, for Your forgiveness of my sins, and for giving me to Jesus. Thank you, Jesus, for coming into my heart to make my heart your habitation (dwelling place forever). Father in Heaven, thank You that you have made me fit for Heaven complete in Jesus. Thank you that I have been born-again. Thank you, that through Jesus, I have access to You as my Heavenly Father. I believe, and I am thankful that You have sent God the Holy Spirit into my heart to help and lead me in Your righteousness for godly living. I confess Jesus Christ as my Lord, according to 1 Corinthians 12: 3. I yield to God the Holy Spirit, my Helper. I want to love and serve You for the rest of my life, for Your glory. Praise You. I look forward to living with you in Heaven. In the name of the Lord Jesus Christ, thank you. Amen.

SIGNATURE PAGE FOR YOURSELF

If you have been serious with God, and have prayed to tell God about your heart's desire, then you have been born-again of the Holy Spirit through faith in Jesus, (Galatians 3: 26). You can sign below to help you remember the date and time you received Jesus Christ as your Savior and Lord, and you began eternal life immediately.

____

Sign Your Name

____

Date and Time

CONGRATULATIONS!

Share your faith in Jesus with someone. Share about your recent decision to receive Jesus Christ as the Living God's Way and gift for you to become a child of God, to have a relationship with Him so you are secured to live with Him in Heaven forever. For confessing Jesus before humankind, Jesus will make you known to His Father and before the angels of God in Heaven. You are accepted by God and will be known by Him in Judgment Day; therefore, you will be received into Heaven through your faith in Jesus. Give thanks to God, bless, glorify, and enjoy your God, El-Elyon, which is your Father in Heaven whom you have chosen to believe. You have a personal, peaceful relationship with the Living God (Romans 5: 1). As a Christian you are no longer under the law of sin and death, but under grace (God's favor), (Romans 6: 14; Titus 3: 5-7). The Christian life is not easy, but God promises you the victory by believing in Jesus, (John 4: 4). God holds you in His Hand, and keeps you by His Spirit, who will raise you to live with El-Elyon forever in a body free of disease, sin and tears, (Revelation 21: 4).

SUMMARY OF WHY TO BELIEVE THE LIVING GOD

*Believe the Living God, El-Elyon, for His gift of righteousness: without which you are NOT able to see Heaven.

Romans 4: 3, 23-25 "For what saith the Scripture? Abraham believed God, and it was counted unto him for righteousness," (vs. 3).

"Now it was not written for his sake alone, that it was imputed unto him; but for us also, to whom it shall be imputed, if we believe on Him that raised up Jesus our Lord from the dead; who was delivered for our offenses, and was raised again for our justification," (vs. 23-25).

Through believing on Jesus, you are pardoned from hell through faith in His death on the Cross. You have God's forgiveness for your sins through faith in Jesus' shed blood and death. Through faith in the resurrection of Jesus bodily from the dead for your justification, you have God's promise of life. You are now secured by your faith in Jesus by God's grace for your eternal home in heaven. When you believe God, His promise of Salvation to you is when you receive and believe on Jesus Christ His Only begotten Son. He declares you as righteous for believing and obeying Him. God welcomes you as his adopted child fitted through Jesus for Heaven. Guaranteed, you will never face condemnation and the second death by believing in Jesus Christ, (John 11: 26-27). Love the Living Triune God and serve Him with all your heart for His glory. He says that all things work out for good to them that love Him, (Romans 8: 28).

APPENDIX 1: FOLLOWUP

Step 1: Read your Bible daily to learn of God for you to grow spiritually. Read Matthew 11: 28-30. To start, read through the Gospel of John, and the Epistle of 1 John.

Step 2: "Study to show thyself approved unto God, a workman that needeth not to be ashamed, rightly dividing the word of truth, (2 Timothy 2: 15).

Step 3: Pray daily with thanksgiving and praise to God letting your requests be known to Him in your new relationship to your Heavenly Father. The way to rejoicing is to "pray without ceasing," (1 Thessalonians 5:17).

Step 4: Find a good Bible-believing Church where the whole counsel of God's Word is being preached truthfully and faithfully. Hebrews 10: 25a says, "Not forsaking the assembling of ourselves together."

Step 5: Talk with your Bible believing and preaching pastor about:

A) Water baptism- where you are giving a public testimony of your personal salvation.

B) Communion-remembrance of what Jesus has done for you.

C) Church membership and God's blessings for you surrounding Tithing.

D) Loving and Worshipping God through serving Him and fellow members of the Church.

Step 6: Develop a Bible-based conservative evangelical theology for your Christian Life. Books that may help you get started are *ABBA'S OWN,* published and displayed on Amazon, or *BREAK FREE FROM TURMOIL soon to be published.* *ABBA'S OWN* has an extensive literature review and bibliographical base to assist you. You may contact the author at the email address given at the end of this booklet.

Step 7: You can say with the Psalmist, "The Lord is my rock, and my fortress, and my deliverer; my God, my strength, in whom I will trust; my buckler, and the horn of my salvation, and my high tower," (Psalms 18: 2). You will want to trust, obey, and give thanks to God daily.

Step 8: When things happen to go wrong, don't blame God and turn your back on Him, He does not cause evil. Start to praise Him more. You need His love and grace more then.

Step 9: Parents and Grandparents train up your children in the way they should go, and when they are older, they shall not depart from it, (Proverbs 22: 6). What the Living God commands us, thou shalt teach them unto our children and grandchildren, when you sit down in thy house, and when you walk by your way, and when you lie down to sleep. Your Bible needs to be an open book read in your house daily, (Deuteronomy 6: 7-8).

Father's provoke not your children to anger, lest they be discouraged, (Ephesians 6:4; Colossians 3: 21).

Step 10: God says, Husbands love your wives, and wives reverence your husbands, (Ephesians 5: 25, 33; 1 Peter 3: 7).

Step 11: Remember God's priority; two commandments 1) Love the Lord your God with all your being, and 2) Love your neighbor as yourself, (Matthew 22: 37-39; Mark 12: 31; Luke 11: 27; John 13: 34). God says you shall be known by your love; love of God and love of your neighbor, (John 13: 35; Romans 5: 5).

In His Word God gives instructions for godly relationships: with Himself, with your spouses, your family, and your neighbors. Search the Bible.

Step 12: Choose to let the Holy Spirit, given to you at the same time as your Salvation by the Father, have full control of you for the enjoyment of new life, not your old sinful nature. The Holy Spirit knows the will of the Father for bearing fruit in your new life, (John 15: 5). In everything give thanks to God, (Philippians 4: 6; I Thess 5: 18).

CHRISTIAN HOPE LIES IN THE RESURRECTION

Jesus is coming again. The Apostle Paul says, in dying you are free from sin, (Romans 6: 7). Also, God says, "But if the Spirit of Him that raised up Jesus from the dead dwell in you, He that raised up Christ from the dead shall also quicken your mortal bodies by His Spirit that dwelleth in you," (Romans 8: 11). On Resurrection Day, you will be raised up unto life in Christ in heaven, forevermore. Jesus is Life, for now, and eternity. Choose Life. Do you confess that by receiving Jesus, He gave you eternal life, immediately? You have been born again. If your answer is "yes," share (confess) this truth with someone else, so they may have the same hope as you. Philippians 2: 11, you may confess Jesus as your Lord, now. 1 John 4: 2, "Every spirit that confesseth that Jesus is come in the flesh is of God." You have a glorious hope that because Christ was raised bodily from the dead on your behalf for your justification, you will be raised bodily unto eternal life, permanently, for your enjoyment of God for His glory and praise. Have you chosen life through faith in Jesus Christ? If your answer is "Yes," then live in the peace of God. God's view of you now is great. You can read about your greatness in God's eyes in Romans 5. Not the easy life, but for you, the Great Life has just begun. The just shall live the Great Life by Faith in Jesus Christ our Savior and Lord.

Other books by Dr David R Lumsden

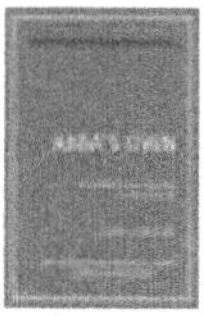

ABBA'S OWN **– A Qualitative Research Study using a case for data collection to verify thesis. The case study is intriguing.**

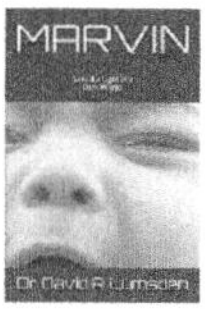

MARVIN **– The story of an unwanted child, allowed to live, excelled beyond expectations for his life. See how you can achieve your desires for your life, too.**

Marvin Sees the Light in a Dark World **shows how Marvin's life was transformed, ending in a victory for a life allowed to live.**

Your copy is available in the Amazon.com Bookstore. Check out all the books available by this author.

All Scripture passages have been taken from the Holy Bible, King James Version, 1971

CONTACT AUTHOR

drdavidrlumsden@gmail.com

Type "Child of God" in the Subject area of your email.

ISBN: 978-1-7773745-4-9

NIICOL Publishing

2020

Made in the USA
Middletown, DE
06 November 2020

23411046R00056